MW01233507

INVESTING

For

BEGINNERS

2020

COMPLETE GUIDE TO

STOCK INVESTMENT

BY Henry Price

TABLE OF CONTENTS

INTRODUCTION TO STOCKS

Stocks are the shares of shareholders. They hold a stock certificate to claim that they can participate in the company's assets and income. History has shown that investing in stocks is one of the most effective and efficient ways for people to create wealth and increase their residual income. Investing in stocks is difficult. As a result, stocks are still misunderstood by some people. The company, where to invest and which stocks to buy are the factors that must be considered before investing in stocks. Therefore, usually, there are two types of shares: ordinary shares and preferred shares. When people talk about stocks, they usually refer to common stocks. The vast majority of socks are produced in this form. They have the right to claim profit (dividends) and have the right to vote.

Preference shares generally have no voting rights. Also unlike ordinary shares, they receive a guaranteed fixed dividend that results in variable dividends that vary over the period depending on the company's earnings or profits. Investing is risky. You must enrich your investment strategy and act tactically to maintain your investment and achieve your desired goals. Thus, investing is "working smarter, not harder".

Stocks and their Background

A stock is a type of security which shows the ownership in the company and the right to a portion of the assets and profits in a company. It is also referred to as **"shares"**.

This is used the ownership of the investor in the company. Those who own shares are usually referred to as shareholders. As a shareholder, an investor theoretically owns a percentage of everything in a company has. The profitability or the absence of the company determines whether its shares are traded at a higher or lower   price.

It is spent by companies to raise capital for the development of a company or the implementation of new projects. The capital (also known as stock) of a company is made up of the shares of its owners. A separate share shows the fractional ownership in the company's participation with the total number of shares.

The stocks of the company are divided into shares, the total amount of which is stated at the time of starting the business. Additional shares are authorized to exist shareholders and issued by the company. In some countries, each share has a certain declared par value, which is the nominal book value used to represent stock on the company's balance sheet. In other countries, however, shares can be issued without par value.

Classes of Shares

In business, there may different types (or classes) of shares, each of which has its own rules of ownership, privileges or the value of shares. Ownership of shares may be documented by issuing a certificate of socks.

A stock certificate is a legal document that specifies the number of shares of the shareholder and other characteristics of the shares, e.g. B. the nominal value (if available) or the share class. Typically, stocks are in the form of common stock or preferred stock.

The difference between the two will be discussed as follows:

Common Stock usually entitles the holder to vote at general meetings and receive dividends. These are stocks that everyone usually refers to when they use the term in the context of portfolio management or the investment world. Currently, ordinary shares are almost always issued as "fully paid and not valuable", which means that after you purchased them, you will not be forced to collect more money, although this has not always been the case. This means that your potential losses are limited to what you invested if you did not take margin loans.

Preferred Stock has no voting rights, but has higher requirements regarding assets and earnings than common shares and has a legal right to receive a certain amount of dividend payments before dividends can be paid to other shareholders. For example, preferred shareholders receive dividends over common shareholders and take precedence in the event of bankruptcy and liquidation of a company. In addition to the two classes of stocks mentioned above, which are common and often used as the main stock classes when investing on the stock exchange, there are some other categories or classifications of stocks that you should be aware to be familiar with them that what investment means.

The other classifications of shares of the stock were given below based on stocks' ownership rights, company specifics, and on their relative size.

Different Types of Stocks and Stock Classifications

1.   Based on Ownership Rights

For classifying stocks the issuing company decides whether to issue common, preferred or hybrid shares. Investors can own two different types of shares. They have different property rights and different privileges.

➢ **Common Stock**

Common stocks, it sounds ordinary. Speaking of stocks, they usually refer to common stocks and the vast majority of shares issued have this form. Common shares represent the ownership of the company and the right to a portion of the profits (dividends) of this company. Investors can also vote to elect the board members who oversee key management decisions. In the past, common stocks had higher returns than almost any other common asset class. In addition to the highest returns, common stocks are also likely to involve the highest risk. If a company goes bankrupt, common shareholders will only receive money when lenders, bondholders and preferred shareholders receive a payment.

This risk can be significantly reduced by owning many different established companies (diversification) with solid statements and a history of strong earnings.

➢ Preferred Stock

Preferred stocks represent a certain degree of ownership of a company, but usually do not have the same voting rights as common stocks. In the case of Preferred stocks, investors are usually guaranteed a fixed dividend. Keep in mind that this is different than common stocks with variable dividend payments that fluctuate with the company's profit.

Unlike common stocks, preferred stocks do not show the same increase (or decrease in value in the event of market downturns) in the price of shares, which leads to a decrease in overall profitability. One of the advantages of preferred stocks is that preferred shareholders are paid to the common shareholder (but still after debtors) in the event of bankruptcy. I like to think that preferred stocks are somewhere between bonds and common stocks. He resembles both. As a result, I would not hold any preference shares. I see no reason to abandon the growth potential of common stocks or the added security of bonds.

2. Based on Company Specifics

Every company have very good plans for growth and dividend distributions which are reflected in these stock classifications.

➤ **Blue-Chip Stocks**

Blue-chip stocks are stocks of the largest companies in the country. Usually, these are high-quality companies with long-term stable profit and stable dividend payments. They are also one of the safest investment stocks because companies are big and stable.

Investments don't have many growth opportunities. This usually leads to stable stock prices, but less for investors. As a result, historical profits for very large companies follow the sales of smaller companies.

➤ **Income Stocks**

Income stocks are uses some time to relate to "Blue Chip" stocks. These are stable companies that pay high dividends. Older investors often buy stocks of these companies with a stable income as this gives them a stable stream of income in the form of. When you combine dividend payments with higher stock prices, these stocks often give a steady rise in stocks prices and give more money to the inverters. This is of course due to the increased risk that the share price will fall in a market downturn.

➢ Value Stocks

Value stocks are the stocks of companies that have the following things given below:

❖ They have low price to earnings ratios

❖ They have a low price to book ratios

❖ They have a low price to dividend ratios

❖ They have a low price to sales-and-cash-flow ratios

In other words, they are underestimated in comparison with other similar companies in the market. Sometimes this is the result of difficulties or financial problems. In other cases, this may be due to investor behaviour and cyclical trends.

➢ Growth Stocks

Growth stocks are the stocks of companies with fast-growing returns. This increase in profits and this is reflected in the increase in the company's share price. These companies often reinvest profits and pay little to shareholders. At the same time, they hope that the growth in the share price will be sufficient to keep shareholders on board.

Growing companies are often technology-oriented and usually either sell the product or focus on research and development. Most of these companies are growing rapidly. The prices of your stocks often rise faster than the basic profit, which leads to a high price-earnings ratio.

This may take some time, but stock prices continue to return to the average historical P / E ratio, so some investors have to burn these stocks. Stock growth can quickly rise in value but often falls even faster.

3. Based on size

Market capitalization is simply a way of specifying the size of a company so that companies can be compared across industries. You calculate market capitalization by multiplying the number of shares issued by the current share price. For example, if a company had 100 million common shares and a current stock price of $ 50 per share, its market capitalization would be $ 5 billion ($ 100 million x $ 50).

Investors categorize companies under these labels. There is no universal agreement on the exact cut-offs.

❖ **Mega-cap:** Over $200 billion investments
❖ **Large-cap:** Over $10 billion investments
❖ **Mid-cap:** $2 billion–$10 billion investments
❖ **Small-cap:** $250 million–$2 billion investments
❖ **Micro-cap:** Below $250 million investments
❖ **Nano-cap:** Below $50 million investments

Company size is very important for stock prices. Investors often refer to mutual funds as small, medium, or large capitalization funds. This means that the mutual fund invests only in companies of a certain size.

There is a strong correlation between risk and profitability. Small companies are riskier than large ones because they have fewer resources, are not established in the market, and may not be as famous as huge issuers of stocks.

Due to the increased risk, these small-cap companies generated higher returns than the small and medium-cap companies for a century. By continuing the trend, medium-cap stocks outperformed large-cap and mega-cap stocks.

For this reason, many investors prefer to allocate a larger portion of their portfolio to small or mid-cap stocks, also known as "tilt". This leads to a slightly higher risk.

Stock CREATION AND ITS EXISTENCE

Stocks have several reasons for existence but the following are

the important reasons:

Stocks allow companies to raise capital (money) to turn good ideas into viable companies, which ultimately benefits civilization. Without capitalism and well-functioning capital markets, most of the modern conveniences you take for granted would not exist or be inaccessible to you.

Shares offer investors the opportunity to achieve a satisfactory return on investment, which enables them to achieve their financial goals faster than usual.

Separates stock ownership and management allows those who do not have an interest, opportunity or time to do business or can continue to participate in economic activities and with the right to vote, which leads to a more efficient allocation of resources, including human capital.

STOCK MARKET HISTORY

In today's world, people want to have a lot of money simply.

Therefore, they want to make profits without further efforts, e.g. For example, running a company, working in a manufacturing company, working in a company with a large number of tasks, etc.

A stock market is a collection of buyers and sellers that represent property rights for companies. These can be securities that are quoted on a public stock exchange, as well as those that are traded only privately.

The stock exchange is a place where buyers and sellers of shares meet and choose the price to trade. Some exchanges are physical locations where transactions are carried out on the trading venue. However, exchanges often become virtual and consist of computer networks in which transactions are carried out and recorded in electronic form.

These are secondary markets where existing stockholders can do business with potential buyers. Therefore, when you buy shares on the stock exchange, you do not buy them from the company, but from some other existing shareholders. Similarly, when you sell, you are not selling your shares directly to the company, but to some other investors who are interested in your shares.

Examples of this are shares of private companies that are sold to investors via crowdfunding platforms. Common stock and other types of securities such as corporate bonds and convertible bonds are listed on the stock exchanges.

Stock markets are one of the important parts of the modern global economy. Some countries use the stock market to grow their economies. Today, stock markets have become a driving force in the country.

Early Stock and Commodity Markets

The first real stock markets did not appear until the 16th century. However, some markets are similar to stock markets. For example, it turned out that there is a system in France in which couriers manage agricultural debt nationwide on behalf of banks. This can be seen as the first important example of brokerage since men are effectively dealing with debt.

Also, the merchants of Venice were later credited with trading in government securities back in the 13th century.

Coffee Shops: First Real Stock Markets

Before investors roared through trading floors and tossed order forms into the air, they were doing business in coffee shops. As the volume of shares traded increased, an organized market for the exchange of these shares was required. As a result, stockbrokers decided to meet in a London cafe that they used as a trading platform. Eventually, they purchase the coffee house and changed its name to "stock exchange" in 1773.

The first stock exchange was founded, the London Stock Exchange. The idea came to the American colonies with an exchange that began in Philadelphia in 1790.

In other words, coffee houses were the first real stock markets as investors visited these markets to buy and sell stocks. Soon, someone realized that the whole business world would become more efficient if someone created their market, where business people could trade stocks without ordering coffee or shouting in a crowded cafe.

The First Stock Exchange

As previously mentioned, a cafe in London became widely known as the first stock exchange and was referred to as the London Stock Exchange. However, this purpose was for government purposes only and the distribution of the country's debts in some other countries. In other words, the holdings are unknown until 1817.

The New York Stock Exchange (NYSE) was founded in 1817 and is an important moment in history. He has been trading stocks since day one. The NYSE is one of the world's leading stock markets along with the NYSE. The Group's stock exchange trades in more US stocks than any other stock exchange.

Unlike some others, however, the NYSE was not the first stock exchange in the United States. The Philadelphia Stock Exchange has this title. However, the NYSE has become the country's most powerful stock exchange due to the lack of internal competition and its position at the centre of US trade and economy in New York.

Modern Stock Markets

Currently, each country has its stock market. Equity markets can be found all over the world, and the global importance of equity markets is underlined. Trillions of dollars are traded every day on stock markets around the world and they are indeed the driving force behind the capitalist world.

In the Philippines, the stock exchange was widely known as Philippine Stock Exchange, Inc... This is the national exchange of the Philippines. It was founded in 1992 through a combination of the Manila Stock Exchange and the Makati Stock Exchange. Including earlier forms, it has been in operation since 1927.

There are many exchanges or stocks markets around the world.

Here are the top 10 stock markets in the world sorted by market capitalization:

- ❖ New York Stock Exchange
- ❖ NASDAQ
- ❖ Tokyo Stock Exchange
- ❖ London Stock Exchange Group
- ❖ Euronext
- ❖ Hong Kong Stock Exchange
- ❖ Shanghai Stock Exchange
- ❖ Toronto Stock Exchange
- ❖ Frankfurt Stock Exchange
- ❖ Australian Securities Exchange

PHILIPPINE STOCK EXCHANGE (PSE)

As previously mentioned, the Philippine Stock Exchange, Inc. (PSE) is the Philippine National Stock Exchange. It was founded on December 23, 1992, and 24 years have passed since the merger of the two exchanges (Manila Stock Exchange and Makati Stock Exchange).

However, it has been in operation since 1927 and has been in operation for 90 years.

In June 1998, the Securities and Exchange Commission (SEC) issued PSE has the status of a "self-regulatory organization" (SRO), which means that it can implement its own rules and set penalties for defective bidders (TPs) and listed companies.

On March 25, 1994, PSE introduced an automated trading system that connects the two exchanges. The system resulted in a uniform trading price for all listed securities as well as in Makati Stock Exchange and the Manila Stock Exchange into PSE. PSE is currently trading shares in two trading areas: one in Makati City and one in Pasig City.

In 2001, PSE was transformed from a non-profit organization led by non-joint-stock companies, shareholders, a revenue-generating company led by the president and board of directors.

STOCK MARKET CONCEPT

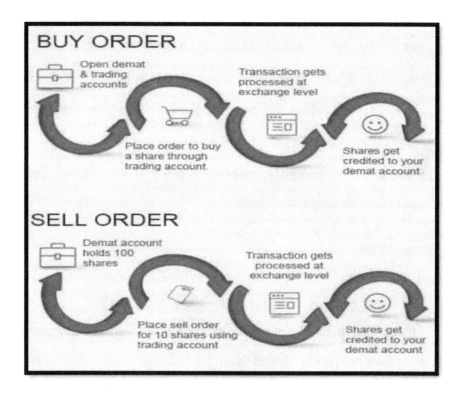

BROKERS

Brokers can be individuals who work for such firms and some time works in the company. Investors can buy stock directly from the company who issues them to purchase but for this, you still need a broker. Although the primary task of brokers is the buying and selling of securities such as stocks.

They can perform other tasks for you who include the following:

Limited banking services offers: Brokers offers interest-bearing accounts, check writing, direct deposit, and credit cards.

Brokering other securities: Brokers can buy bonds, mutual funds, options, Exchange Traded Funds (ETFs) and other investments on your behalf.

Personal stockbrokers can make money their various fees which also includes the following:

Commissions of the broker: Broker commission consist of the fee for buying and/or selling stocks and other securities.

Charges of interest: Interest is getting through investors for borrowing their brokerage account for investment purposes.

Charges of the service: Charges for the service are for performing administrative tasks and other functions.

Broker which is dealing with you should be registered with the National Association of Securities Dealers (NASD) and Exchange Commission (SEC). To protect your money after you deposit it into your brokerage account, the broker must be a member of the Securities Investors Protection Corporation (SIPC).

SIPC does not protect you from market losses. It protects your money if the brokerage goes bankrupt. Contact NASD, SEC, and SIPC to find out if a broker is registered with these organizations.

The distinction between private and institutional stockbrokers is important. Institutional brokers earn money from institutions and enterprises through investment banking services and fees for the placement of securities, consulting services and other brokerage services. Personal brokers offer the same services to individuals and small enterprises.

Distinguishing between Full-Service and Discount Brokers

Stockbrokers are of two categories: **Full-service** and **Discount brokers**.

The type you choose depends on what type of investor you are. In short, full-service brokers are suitable for investors who need guidance, while discount brokers are more suitable for investors who are confident enough and knowledgeable about equity investments to manage them with minimal help. Full-service broker Full-service brokers are what the name indicates. They try to offer as many services as possible to investors who open accounts with them. When you open an account with a brokerage firm, a representative will be assigned to your account. This agent is commonly referred to by a brokerage firm as a customer service manager, registered agent, or financial advisor.

SERVICE PROVIDED BY BROKER

Full-service brokers can provide you:

Offer guidance and advice. The biggest difference between full-service brokers and discount brokers is the personal attention you get from your agent in your account. You get the first person's name from a full-service broker and reveal a lot of information about your finances and financial goals. The representative should make recommendations on stocks and funds. Full-service brokers can give you access to your investment research.

This information can be very valuable but keep in mind about pitfalls.

Help you achieve your investment goals. In addition to recommendations for certain investments, a good representative gets to know you and your investment objectives, then offers advice and answers your questions about how certain investments and strategies can help you achieve your asset objectives.

Make investment decisions on your behalf. Many investors do not want to be bothered when making investment decisions. Full-service brokers may make decisions for your account with your consent. This service is good, but make sure they explain your choice.

IMPORTANT THINGS TO REMEMBER

Full-service brokers can make life easy for an investor but remember some important points to avoid problems:

➢ Brokers and accounts representatives are sellers. No matter how well they treat you, they still get compensation based on their ability to generate income for the brokerage firm. They generate commissions from you on behalf of the company.

➢ When your employee makes a proposal or recommendation, be sure to ask for a reason and request a complete answer that includes reasons for the recommendation. A good consultant can clearly explain the reasons for each proposal. If you do not fully understand and agree with the advice, do not accept it.

➢ Full-service broker costs more than working with a discounted broker. Discount brokers are only paid to buy or sell stocks for you. Full-service brokers do this and more. They also offer tips and tricks. Because of this, full-service brokers are more expensive. Besides, most full-service brokers expect you to invest at least $ 5,000 to $ 10,000 to open an account.

➢ Giving decision or making authority to your representatives can be negative, as it is always difficult to make other financial decisions for you, especially when they use your money. If they make the wrong investment decisions that make you lose money, you may not be able to seek help because you allowed them to act on your behalf.

➢ Some brokers engage in activities called churning. Churning is the buying and selling of shares for the sole purpose of receiving commissions. Churning is good for brokers, but bad for customers. If your account is very active, ask for a reason. Commissions, especially with full-service brokers, can significantly affect your assets. Therefore, do not tolerate any runoff or other suspicious actions.

➢ Before dealing with a broker (a full-service broker, or another broker) you can get a free broker report from the National

Association of Securities Dealers by calling 800-289-9999 or on the NASD website at www.nasdr. Com. The report may indicate whether complaints or sanctions have been filed against this brokerage firm or individual representative.

> Merrill Lynch and Morgan Stanley are examples of a full-time broker. Of course, all brokers now have fully-featured websites where you can get additional information about their services. Get as much information as you can before opening your account.

Discount brokers

As the name suggests, discount brokers are cheaper to win than full-service brokers. Investors should know about their personal goals and needs before start working with discount brokers. You have a great responsibility to do adequate research to make the right choice of stocks and you should be willing to accept the result, regardless of what the result is.

The regular investor had two types of discount brokers to choose: **conventional discount brokers** and **Internet discount brokers**. **Conventional discount brokers** ran most of their business through regular offices and over the phone, while online discount brokers did most of their business through websites. Thanks to industry consolidation, most traditional discount brokers now have full-featured websites, while online discount brokers have been set up by adding additional phone and personal services.

SERVICES PROVIDED BY DISCOUNT BROKERS

Discount brokers offer some significant advantages such as:

Lower costs: Lower costs are usually the result of lower fees and the main benefit of using discount brokers.

Impartial service: Discount brokers offer you the opportunity to only carry out transactions for the purchase and sale of shares. Since they don't give advice, they're not interested in selling you a particular stock.

Access to information: Installed discount brokers offer extensive training materials in their offices or on their websites.

BEFORE YOU START BUYING

Before choosing a broker, you need to analyze your investment style. Once you know yourself and how you invest, you can find the type of broker that suits your needs.

When choosing a broker, keep the following points in mind:

Choose your investment style with a brokerage firm that charges the lowest amount for the services you are likely to use most often.

Compare all costs of buying, selling, storing stocks and other securities through a broker. Don't just compare commissions. Compare other expenses such as interest margin and other service fees.

Discovering Various Types of Brokerage Accounts

If you choose to invest in the stock market, you have to pay for the stocks you buy. Most brokerage firms offer investors different types of accounts, each of which serves its purpose. In the following sections, I present the three most common types.

The main difference is how certain brokers evaluate your "creditworthiness" when buying and selling securities. If you have a bad balance, you can only choose a cash account. If you have a good balance, you can open a cash or margin account. Once you have received the right to a margin account, you can update it to trade options.

To open an account, you must complete an application and send a check or money order, at least the minimum amount required to open an account.

Cash accounts

A cash account means exactly what you think. You will need to deposit the amount of money with the new account application to start trading. The amount of your first deposit varies from broker to broker. Some brokers have a minimum of $ 10,000, while others allow you to open an account for as little as $ 500. From time to time you can see a broker offering no deposit cash accounts, usually as part of a promotion.

If you have a cash account, your money must be credited to the account before the closing date of a transaction you have made. Closing takes place three working days after the transaction date (due date). You may need to have money in your account before the due date. See Chapter 6 for details on this and other important data.

If you have money in a brokerage account, find out if the broker pays you interest on money that is not invested. Some offer a service where non-invested money places money market bets, and you can even choose whether the venue is a regular money account or a tax-free municipal money market account.

Margin accounts

A margin account allows you to borrow money against securities in the account to buy more shares. Since you can borrow on a margin account, you must be qualified and approved by a broker. Once you have been approved, this recently found loan gives you more leverage so you can buy more stocks or make short sales. The margin limit for share trading is 50 per cent.

For example, if you want to buy shares worth $ 10,000 in the margin, you must have at least $ 5,000 cash in your account. Most brokers typically charge an interest rate that is several points above the loan rate.

Margin is a stock, that is, a mortgage for the purchase of the real estate. You can buy real estate for cash, but it often makes sense to use borrowed funds, as you may not have enough money to buy 100% in cash, or prefer not to pay all the cash. For example, with a mark-up, you can buy stocks for $ 10,000 for only $ 5,000. The rest of the stock purchase is acquired through a loan (margin) from a brokerage firm.

Option accounts

An optional account offers you all the functions of a margin account as well as the option to trade stock options and stock indices. To upgrade your margin account to an options account, the broker typically asks you to sign a statement that you know the options and are familiar with the risks involved. Options can be a very effective addition to a range of investment tools.

JUDGING BROKER SUGGESTIONS

In recent years, Americans have fallen in love with a new stock brokerage in television financial shows. In these shows, a neat market strategist often talks about a particular stock. It is known that some stocks grow significantly immediately after influential analysts give recommendations on the purchase. The speculations and opinions of analysts are very funny and many people take their views very seriously. However, most investors should be very careful when analysts, especially those curious on TV, make recommendations.

Brokers give their recommendations as a general idea of how much they relate to a particular stock. The following list contains the most important recommendations for you:

Strong purchases:

The analyst loves this choice, and it would be very reasonable for you to buy several stocks. However, keep in mind that buying recommendations are probably the most common as brokers sell stocks.

Accumulated and the market developed:

The analyst who makes this type of recommendation is positive, but not interested in the choice. This rating is similar to asking a friend if they like your new suit and getting a "nice" answer in a monotonous voice. This is a polite answer, but you want his opinion to be more enthusiastic.

Sell:

Many analysts were supposed to make this recommendation in 2000 and 2001, but few did. So many investors lost money because some analysts were too good or just afraid, to be honest and sound the alarm and push people to sell.

Avoid the plague:

I'm just joking about it, but I want this recommendation to be available. I have seen many stocks that I think we're a terrible investment - stocks of companies that made no money and were in a terrible financial situation that should never be considered. However, investors absorb billions of dollars of stock that will ultimately become worthless.

Do not get me wrong:

An analyst's recommendation is certainly better advice than what you would get from your hairdresser or your sister-in-law's neighbour, but you want to see analyst recommendations with a healthy dose of reality. Analysts are biased because their employment depends on the companies that are represented. Please note that analyst recommendations can play a useful role in your analysis of equity investments. If you find a great promotion, and then analysts give brilliant reports on the same promotion, you are on the right track!

Buy and sell stocks using your brokerage account

Regardless of the type of brokerage mechanism used, the mechanism for buying or selling shares is fairly consistent. First, the stock price is received. In the early days of stock exchanges, price information was transmitted through a ticker-tape - a long paper tape that printed basic data using a telegraph wire. That is why we still call stock market prices tickers. A stock price contains a lot of information, including the current bid price and the price, as well as the last traded price. An offer is the highest price that someone in the market is currently willing to pay, and an offer is the lowest price that someone is willing to sell. If you are interested in buying stocks and want to sell an offer then bid. If the bid and offer prices match, this affects the business.

Stock quotes are often real-time quotes that contain detailed information about seconds, and online quotes often include charts and interactive tools. Stocks are listed, for example, for Ayala Corporation (AC) and Mega world Corporation (MEG) with their ticker symbol.

In this regard, investors should have some knowledge of how to interpret the stock movements of the company they have acquired to manage investments and properly manage their investments with their skills, abilities and understanding.

How to the interpretation of the stock table

The given below is the interpretation of the stock table to understand:

Stock Tables

52-W(High)	52-W(Low)	Name(Symbol)	Div	Volume	Yld	P/E	Last Day	Net Chg
21.50	8.00	SkyHigh.Corp		3,143		76	21.25	+.25
47.00	31.75	LowDown.Inc	2.35	2,735	5.9	18	41.00	−.50
25.00	21.00	ValueNow.Inc	1.00	1,894	4.5	12	22.00	+.10
83.00	33.00	DoinBadly.Corp		7,601			33.50	−.75

Columns 1 (52W-high)

52-Wk High gives tells the highest price that particular stock has reached in the most recent 52-week period. If the company is strong, it may be a good opportunity to buy the stock at a lower price. Avoid the company having tough times.

Columns 2 (52W-low)

The column labelled "52-Wk Low" gives you the lowest price that particular stock reached in the most recent 52-week period. The high and the low prices give you a range stock's price has moved within the past 52 weeks. The company could alert you that a stock has problems, or they could tell you that a stock's price has fallen enough to make it a bargain. Simply reading the 52-Wk High and 52-Wk Low columns aren't enough to determine which of those two scenarios is happening. They tell you to get more information before you commit your money.

Column 3(Company Name & Type of Stock)

This column lists the name of the company. Common stock doesn't have any special symbols or letters in the name. When you have your eye on stock for potential purchase, get familiar with its symbol. If you know this symbol, you can easily find your shares in financial tables where the shares are listed alphabetically by company name. Stock symbols are the language for investing in stocks and you need to use them to trade stocks from getting a stock price in your broker's office to buying stocks online. Symbols represent different classes of shares in the stock. Like "pf" means the shares are preferred stock.

Column 4(Ticker Symbol)

The ticker is the unique alphabetic name to identify the stock. When you watch financial television, you see how the ticker moves on the screen and shows the latest prices next to this symbol. When searching for stock quotes on the Internet, the company is used using the ticker symbol.

Column 5(Dividend per Share)

Dividend per share indicates the annual payment of dividends per share. If this area is empty, the company does not currently pay dividends. Dividends are payments to owners (shareholders). When a company pays dividends, it is displayed in the dividend column. The amount you see is the annual dividend that is indicated for one share of this share. If you look at Low Down.Inc (LDI), you can see that you get $2.35 as an annual dividend for each share of stock that you own. Companies usually pay the dividend in quarterly amounts. If I own 100 shares of LDI, the company pays me a quarterly dividend of $58.75 ($235 total per year).

A healthy company seeks to maintain or increase dividends for shareholders from year to year. In any case, the dividend is very important for investors who want to receive income from equity investments.

Column 6(Dividend Yield)

The dividend yield is the percentage return on the dividends. It is calculated as an annual dividend per share divided by the price per share. Profitability is generally the return on the money you invest.

In the stock tables, however, the return shows the percentage of this particular dividend at the share price. Profitability is most important for investor income. Dividing the annual dividend by the current share price gives you the dividend yield. Please note that many companies reported no returns. Since they have no dividends, income is zero. Please note that the yield on the finance pages changes daily as stock prices change. Refunds are always reported as if you were buying stocks that day. If you buy VNI on the day indicated in the table above, your return will be 4.5 per cent. Investors who buy shares at $ 30 per share will receive a return of only 3.3 per cent. Of course, since you bought stocks at $ 22, you essentially set your previous return at 4.5 per cent.

Column 7(Price/Earnings Ratio)

The price ratio is calculated by dividing the current share price by earnings per share for the past four quarters. The P / E are the ratio between the share price and the company's profit. The P/E is widely recognized and an important value barometer in the world of equity investments. P / E is often used to determine if a stock is expensive. Value investors believe that the P / E ratio is necessary to analyze the share as a potential investment. As a rule, the P / E ratio for stocks with large capitalization or income should be from 10 to 20. P

/ E ratio of not more than 30-40 is preferred for growth stocks. In the P / E ratio specified in the share tables, the price refers to the value of one share. Earnings refer to the company's earnings per share for the past four quarters. The P / E is the price divided by the profit. In the table above, the VNI has a P / E of 12, which is considered a low P / E. SHC has a relatively high P / E. This stock is considered too expensive because you pay a price that is 76 times more profit. DBC does not have an available P / E ratio. Typically, this lack of P / E indicates that the company reported losses over the past four quarters.

Column 8(Trading Volume)

Trading volume indicates the total number of shares traded for the day and it is listed in hundreds. To get the actual number of sells, add "00" at the end of the numbers. When you hear the word volume in the news, it usually refers to how many stocks are bought and sold for the entire market.

Of course, it's important to keep an eye on the volume as the stocks you invest in are somewhere in this activity. The volume refers to a single share in the "Volume" column in the table above. The volume indicates how many shares of this particular share were sold on that day. If only 100 shares are traded per day, the trading volume is 100. On the trading day specified in the table, SHC passed into the hands of 3,143 shares. As a rule, business news media only mention the volume of a particular stock if it is unusually large. When a stock usually has a volume in the range of 5,000 to 10,000 and the trading volume suddenly reaches 87,000, it is time to sit down and pay attention. You can't necessarily compare the volume of stock to the volume of another company. Highly capitalized stocks such as IBM or Microsoft typically trade millions of shares almost daily, while less active smaller stocks can have an average trading volume in much smaller amounts.

The main thing to remember is that trading volume is much higher than the normal range of this stock is a sign that something is happening with this stock. It may be negative or positive, but something new is happening with this company. If the news is positive, an increase in volume is the result of more and more people buying stocks, and if the news is negative, an increase in volume is likely the result of an increase in the number of people selling stocks.

Some reasons are given below that can cause increased trading volume:

New business deal: Every company announces new business deals like a joint venture or lands a big client.

Indirect benefits from company: A company benefit from new development in the economy or from a new law passed by the government.

Reasons for a decline in trading volume for a particular stock are given below:

Bad earnings: Profit is the lifeblood of a company. When a company's profits fall or disappear, you see more volume.

Problems of governments: The stock is being targeted by government action (such as a lawsuit or Securities and Exchange Commission probe).

Issues of liabilities: The media report that a company has a defective product or a similar problem.

Column 9 and 10(Day High and Low)

Day High and Low indicate the price range at which the stock has traded throughout the day. Both columns show maximum and the minimum prices that people have paid for the stock.

Column 11(Close)

Close is the last transaction price set on the day at which market close? If the closing price is more than 5% higher or lower than the previous day's closing price then the entire listing of this share is shown in bold. Keep in mind that if you buy shares the next day, you are not guaranteed to get the same price because of the price changes constantly (even after the stock exchange closes during the day). The closing is only an indication of past performance and except for extreme circumstances. It serves as a rough indication of what you have to pay.

Column 12(Net Change)

Net change is the dollar value change in the stock price from the previous day's closing price. The net change was positive when you hear about a stock being "up for the day".

Using News about Dividends

Reading and understanding dividend reports are very important if you are an income investor. When you look at key dates to understand how buying dividend stocks can benefit you as an investor, you need to know how companies report and pay dividends.

Some important dates in a dividend are given below:

Declaration Date: This is the date when a company reports a quarterly dividend and the subsequent payment dates. The date of declaration is just the announcement date. If you buy the stock before, on the date of declaration, it won't matter regarding receiving the stock's quarterly dividend.

Date of execution: This is the day you initiate the stock transaction. If you call up a broker today to buy a particular stock, then today is the date of execution or the date on which you execute the trade.

Date of closing: The closing or settlement date is the date on which the trade is finalized, which usually happens three business days after the date of execution.

Records: The date of record is used to identify which stockholders qualify to receive the declared dividend. The company establishes a cut-off date by declaring date of record.

All investors who are official shareholders on the specified cut-off date will receive dividends on the payment date, even if they plan to sell the stock at any time between the announcement date and the records date.

Ex-dividend date: Ex-dividend means without dividend. Because it takes three days to process a stock purchase before you become an official owner of the stock, you have to qualify before the three days. These three days are known as the "ex-dividend period." If you buy stocks within this short time, you do not get into the accounts because the end date is after the date of receipt.

Payment date: The date on which a company issues and mails its dividend checks to shareholders.

Understanding why these dates matter

Remember that there are three business days between the due date and the due date. Three business days are also between the dividend payment date and the recording date. This information is important to know if you want to qualify for the upcoming dividend. Timing is important, and once you understand this data, you know when to buy stocks and whether you qualify for dividends. Suppose you want to buy Value Now.Inc (VNI) in time to get a quarterly dividend of 25 cents per share. Suppose the shooting date is February 10th.

You must complete the transaction no later than February 7th to determine the dividends. If you comply with the commercial law on February 7, the closing date will come in three days, February 10, in time for the date of admission. So, the close of trading is February 11 after the date of recording. As you are not registered as an official shareholder at the time of registration, you will not receive this quarterly dividend. In this example, the period from February 7th to 10th is called the period without dividends. Fortunately, for those who buy stocks in this short period of earlier dividends, stocks are trading at a lower price to reflect the number of dividends.

STOCK PRICES

The share price also is known as the value of the company. At the simplest level, this value is calculated by dividing the value of the company by the number of shares issued known as market capitalization.

For example, if ABC is worth P1, 000,000 and P1, 00,000 then the shares are outstanding. The price of each share is P10.00.

The company has things to buy and sells. The company also have buildings, cars, patents, money in a bank, etc. '-'represents the book value or the amount of money that the company will receive if it sells all things at once.

ADVANTAGES OF INVESTING IN STOCKS

Investment Gains

One of the main advantages of investing in the stock market is the ability to increase your money. Over time as the stock market tends to increase then the prices of individual stocks also rise. The prices of individual stocks change daily. Investing in stable companies that can grow gives profit to investors.

Stock ownership takes advantage of a growing economy

As the economy grows, corporate profits also grow. This is because economic growth creates income. A thicker salary increases consumer demand which means that more money goes into corporate cash registers. This helps to understand the phases of the business   cycle.

Historically, the average annual return on stocks was 10 per cent. This is better than the average annual inflation rate of 3.2 per cent. This means that you have a longer time horizon. In this way, you can buy and hold even if the value drops temporarily. Compare stocks, inflation, and gold prices are in the gold price history.

Easy to buy

The stock market makes it easy to buy stocks of companies. You can purchase them through a broker, financial planner or online. Once you have created an account, you can buy stocks in a few minutes.

You make money in two ways:

* Most investors intend to buy the stock at a low price and then sell at a high price. You invest in fast-growing companies by checking its value. This is attractive for both traders and investors. The first group hopes to take advantage of short-term trends, while the latter assumes that the company's earnings and share price will increase over time. Both believe that their stock-picking skills allow them to beat the market. Other investors prefer regular cash flows. They buy stocks from companies that pay dividends. These companies are growing moderately.

* They are easy to sell. Selling your shares on the stock exchange at any time is very easy. This is important when you suddenly need money. Since prices are volatile, you run the risk of incurring losses.

DISADVANTAGES OF INVESTING IN STOCKS

You could lose your entire investment

If the company does not work well, investors sell which leads to a decline in the share price. If you sell, you lose your original investment. If you can't afford to lose your original investment, you should buy bonds. You will receive an income tax benefit if you lose money due to the loss of shares. Unfortunately, you also have to pay taxes when you make money.

Stockholders are paid last if the company share gets low. Preferred stockholders and bondholders get paid first while stockholders are paid at last in the case of company breakage.

It requires a lot of time

You must examine each company to determine how profitable it will be before you buy stocks. You need to learn how to read financial statements and annual reports, as well as follow the news of your company.

You also need to monitor the stock market itself, since even the price of the best company will fall in the event of a market correction, market crash or a bear market.

- ❖ It can be an emotional rollercoaster
- ❖ Stock prices rise and fall every second.
- ❖ Individuals can buy high out of greed and sell low out of fear.

You compete against professionals

Individual investors generally missed most of the growth in stock markets. Retail investors have more natural advantages than stock market investors.

The biggest advantage that an individual investor can achieve over professional money managers is time. You have time to watch the development of the business and the growth of its value. You also have time to watch the company skilfully reinvest capital into additional growth opportunities to repay multiple initial investments.

Most institutional investors are modern. They are forced to chase performances and look over their shoulders to make sure that no one is shooting at them. Institutional investors and fund managers with declining performance often see a sharp outflow of funds. Therefore, it is vital for them to always be the hottest stocks.

This often means that they do not have the patience to wait for a big discount to be realized. You cannot wait patiently for the investments to be completed over more than 6-12 months. The biggest problem for institutional investors is that they often have to benefit from high-performance stocks to compensate for their losers and always achieve a net productivity gain.

Individual investors are not required to track short-term results. Individual investors do not have to sell big winners to receive paper profits. The fact that retail investors do this indicates a desire to take profits and a lack of patience in the long run.

In general, managed funds are also subject to an arbitrary position and sector restrictions that limit position sizes. One of the biggest advantages that individual investors have is the ability to add small and medium cap stocks at will without the need to weigh up the portfolio.

In practice, most funds cannot buy enough small or medium-sized stocks to fundamentally change the performance of their funds.

You would have to buy too much from the company to significantly change the performance of the fund. As a sole investor, a strong company with medium-capitalization can significantly affect productivity.

A single investor has great control over his fate. Investors have virtually no choice in buying high and selling low. They replenish managed funds with new money when markets go up and replenish funds with buyback requests when performance is poor.

To maintain the desired weight of shares, fund managers have no choice but to invest the excess money that accumulates as stock prices rise, and, conversely, must sell shares to finance the buyback of investors when stock prices fall.

With a little patience and little discipline, individual investors can manage their own money much better than many funds. The ability to stick with strong winners and hold them for long periods without market pressure to make profits is benefits that most funds don't have.

Investors striving for growth are more likely to see the money that could be distributed because dividends are reinvested in the company, so (we hope) a greater profit is made by increasing or increasing the share price. People who are interested in increasing their wealth see stocks as a convenient way to do so. Equity growth is generally riskier than other categories but offers excellent long-term prospects for making a lot of money. If you are the type of investor who has enough time to make growing risky stocks, or who has enough money so that a loss does not devastate you financially, then stock growth is definitely for you. As they say, no courage, no glory. The challenge is to find out which stocks will make you richer faster.

If you are not starting your own business, investing in stocks is the best way to benefit from doing business. I want to emphasize that you need to remember that you invest in a company to make money with stocks for a long time. Buying shares is just one way to participate in a company's success (or failure).

Invest in stock only if you're just as excited about it as you would be if you were the CEO and in charge of running the company. As the owner of the company, you have a greater interest in investing in stocks. Think you are the owner and be actively interested in the company's products, services, sales, earnings, etc. This attitude and discipline can improve your goals as a stock investor. This approach is particularly important if your investment goal is growth.

Become a Valuable Growth Investor

A stock is considered growing if it grows faster and faster than the entire stock market. Stock growth works better than its competitors in categories such as sales and profits. The value of shares is shared whose price is lower than the value of the company and its assets. You can determine the value of shares by analyzing the fundamentals of the company and looking at key financial indicators, such as value for money. Growing stocks tend to have better growth prospects soon (one to four years), but valuable stocks tend to be less risky and more sustainable in the long run. Over the years, disputes about growth and value investments in the financial world have tacitly surfaced. Some people argue that a large number of people are buying stocks with growth, as they are expected to increase stock prices compared to the current value of the company. For example, investor growth cannot be delayed by a price-earnings ratio of 30, 40, or higher. Valuable investors are too nervous to buy stocks with this P / E ratio.

However, you can have both. A value-based approach to investment growth is best for you. Long-term equity investors analyze the company's core principles to ensure that the company's growth prospects are solid.

When buying stocks, pay attention to the value and analyze the company's growth prospects. Growth includes, but is not limited to, the health and growth of a particular industrial sector and the entire economy.

The bottom line is that growth is much easier to achieve if you are looking for reliable, value-oriented companies in growing industries. As a value-oriented growth investor, he probably has the longest track record of success compared to most other equity investment philosophies. The experience of those who use value-based investment

in growth is enviable. Warren Buffett, Benjamin Graham, John Templeton and Peter Lynch are some of the most famous practitioners. Everyone can have their ideas about the concepts, but they all successfully apply the basic principles of value-based investment in growth for many years.

Tips for Choosing Growth Stocks

When choosing stocks for growth, consider investing in a company only if it is making a profit, understand how it makes the profit and generates revenue.

Making the right comparison

You need to measure the growth of the company with something to find out if it is stock growth. Usually, you compare the growth of one company with the growth of other companies in the same industry or with the stock market as a whole. When you measure stock growth versus the stock market, you compare them to a common benchmark such as the Dow Jones Industrial Average (DJIA) or Standard & Poor's 500.

If the company's earnings growth is 15 per cent per year for three or more years and the average growth rate in the industry is 10 per cent over the same period, that stock is qualified as a growth reserve.

This not only the company is growing but also because the company is doing well with some consistency. A year in which your income is better than the S&P 500 average does not decrease it. Growth must be achieved consistently.

Checking out a company's fundamentals

When you hear the word basics in the world of equity investments, you are listening to the financial condition of the company and the relevant data. When it comes to fundamental analysis, these are the fundamental data of the company, its balance sheet, profit and loss statement, cash flows and other operational data, as well as external relations such as the company's market position, industry and key impacts. Fundamental data provides the correct information about the relationship of the company.

Keep the following points in mind:

Sales: As a decent benchmark, you want to see sales of at least 10 per cent higher than last year. Although it may differ depending on the industry, 10 per-cents is reasonable.

Earnings: Earnings increases at the same rate as sales.

Debt: The death knell of many a company has been excessive debt.

The company's financial situation has many factors but these numbers are the most important. I also understand that using a 10 per cent number seems too easy but you don't have to complicate things unnecessarily.

I know someone's computerized financial model can reach 9.675 per cent, or maybe 11.07 per cent, but stay simple for now.

Looking for leaders and megatrends

Strong Company has great success in a growing industry. If you look at the history of equity investments, this question is constantly being raised. Investors should pay attention to megatrends because they ensure your success.

Megatrend is a serious development that will be of great importance to many of society for a long time. Good examples are the advent of the Internet and America's ageing. Both trends offer significant challenges and opportunities for our economy.

Take at least the Internet. The potential for economical use is still developing. Millions flock there for many reasons. According to the census, over the next 20 years, older people (over 65) will be the fastest-growing segment of our population. After the bear market in 2000-2002, two megatrends peaked: rising energy prices and overheating of the real estate market. As of 2005, these two topics were the latest news with huge wave effects on the country's economy as a whole. The strategy has become clear for a growing investor.

Find value-oriented companies with solid foundations that are well-positioned to capitalize on these megatrends. From 2002 to 2005, many energy and housing stocks jumped. When oil exceeded $ 65 a barrel and gasoline reached $ 3 a gallon, most oil and oilfield services companies saw their reserves increase by 50%, 100% or more over three years. Housing stocks were even more impressive. Companies serving these industries also flourished.

Listed mortgage banks also published impressive results:

❖ Considering a company with a strong niche

❖ Companies that are well established are profitable.

Always search for the company which have the following characteristics:

A company with a strong brand: Companies such as Coca-Cola and Microsoft come to mind. Other companies may make carbonated drinks or software, but companies need far more than a similar product to overthrow companies that have established an almost irrevocable public identity.

High barriers: The United Parcel Service and federal express service has created huge distribution and delivery networks that competitors cannot easily copy. High entry barriers give recognized companies an important advantage.

Noticing whose buying and/or recommending the stock

You can invest in a great company but still, its stock is stable. This is due to the stock goes up in demand having more buyers than sellers of the stock. The things to remember are given below:

Institutional buying: Institutional buying can exert tremendous upward pressure on the stock's price. When a mutual fund buys a stock, others will follow. Despite all the talk about independent research, a herd mentality still exists.

The attention of the analyst: Analyst give you good analyst's recommendations, it offers some positive reinforcement for your stock. Don't ever buy a stock solely based on an analyst's recommendation. Just know that if you buy a stock based on your research, and analysts subsequently rave about it, your stock price is likely to go up.

Consumers: No, you won't find investment advice here. This one seems to come out of the left-field, but it's a source that you should notice. Publications such as customer reports regularly check products and services and evaluate them for customer satisfaction. When company offers are well received by consumers, this is a strong positive outcome for the company. This type of attention ultimately has a positive effect on the company's shares.

Learning investing in history

The growth stock is not a creature like the Loch Ness monster that has always been talked about but has rarely been seen. Equity growth has been part of the financial scene for almost a century. Many examples offer a wealth of information that you can apply to the current situation on the stock exchange. Check out the previous market winners, especially in the 1970s and 1980s. The 1970s were a tough, bearish decade for stocks, while the 1980s was booming. Expertise and logical action are just as important for a successful equity investment as for any other activity.

Choose a company with solid foundations, including signs of increased sales and profits and low debt.

Make sure the company is in a growing industry. During a bull market, when prices on the stock exchange and in the economy as a whole rise, fully invest in stocks. Switch more money from growth stocks to protective stocks during the bear market. Control your stocks. Stick to stocks that continue to rise and sell stocks that are down.

Evaluating the management of a company

The management of a company is crucial for its success. Before you buy shares in a company, you want to know that management does an excellent job. If you call and ask the company, they may not even answer your call. The best way is to check the numbers. If the company's management does business well, the bottom line is an increase in stock prices.

Return on equity

Although there are several ways to measure management effectiveness, you can get a brief overview of the competence of the management team by checking the company's return on equity (ROE). You simply calculate ROE by dividing the result by capital. The percentage received gives a good idea of whether the company uses its capital efficiently and profitably. In principle, the higher the percentage is better. However, you can consider ROE stable if that percentage is 10 per cent or more.

For checking the company's earnings then check the company's income statement. The income statement is a simple financial statement that expresses the equation: sales fewer expenses equal net earnings.

Table 8-1	Grobaby, Inc, Income Statement	
	2005 Income Statement	2006 Income Statement
Sales	$82,000	$90,000
Expenses	−$75,000	−$78,000
Net earnings	$7,000	$12,000

To find out the capital of a company, look at the balance of this company. The balance sheet is a simple annual financial report that represents less total assets. In state-owned corporations, net assets are called "stocks" or simply "stocks."

Table 8-2 shows the balance for Grobaby, Inc

Table 8-2   Grobaby. Inc, Balance Sheet

	Balance Sheet for December 31, 2005	Balance Sheet for December 31, 2006
Total assets (TA)	$55,000	$65,000
Total liabilities (TL)	−$20,000	−$25,000
Equity (TA less TL)	$35,000	$40,000

Table 8-1, shows that Grobaby.Inc profits increased from $ 7,000 to $ 12,000. In Table 8-2, you can see Grobaby.Inc capital increased from $ 35,000 to $ 40,000 a year. ROE 2005 is 20 per cent ($ 7,000 profit divided by $ 35,000 equity), which is a solid indicator. Next year's return on equity is 30 per cent ($ 12,000 profit divided by $ 40,000), which is another solid indicator.

Equity and earnings growth

Two other barometers for success are the company's earnings growth and the capital increases. Look at the sales growth in Table 8-1. A profit increased from $ 7,000 in 2005 to $ 12,000 in 2006, or 71%, which is an excellent measure. In Table 8-2, Grobaby's net worth increased $ 5,000 (from $ 35,000 to $ 40,000), or 14 percent. This is a very good guide that does good things here.

Insider buying

It is important to control management. Another good sign of how well a company works are whether management buys shares in the company. If a company is focused on growth, and management buys up the company's stock in bulk, this is a good sign of the potential of this stock.

Making sure a company continues to do well

The company's financial situation is changing, and as a hardworking investor, you need to keep checking the numbers while the stocks are in your portfolio. You may have chosen a great promotion from a great company with big numbers in 2003, but the numbers have likely changed since then.

Good stocks don't always stay that way. The great choice that will appeal to you today may become an outcast of tomorrow.

Good and bad information moves like lightning. At the end of 2000, analysts saw Enron as a cream product and fell for themselves to praise its virtues. Even in September 2001, Enron named Abby Joseph Cohen, market strategist, as its first choice in the energy sector. However, Enron shocked investors when it declared bankruptcy in December 2001. The stock price fell from $ 84 in December 2000 to an incredible 26 cents per share (X!).

Exploring Small-caps and Speculative Stocks

A small-cap refers to the size of the corporate market. Small-cap stocks are stocks with a market value of less than $ 1 billion. Investors may be at higher risk with low capitalization but also have a chance of making big profits.

Of all types of stocks, small-cap stocks continue to grow the most. Just as a tree planted last year offers more growth opportunities than mature 100-year-old mahogany, small caps have greater growth potential than established stocks of large caps. Of course, the little company does not show impressive growth just because it is small. It grows when it does the right things, such as increasing sales and profits through the production of goods and services that customers want.

For every small business that becomes a Fortune 500 company, hundreds of companies don't grow or stop operating at all. If you're trying to guess the next big stock before there are signs of growth, don't invest in speculation.

Avoid Initial public offerings (IPOs)

IPOs are the birthplace of public shares. An IPO is the first public offering of shares in a company. An IPO is also known as going public. Because a company's IPO is often an unproven company, investing in an IPO can be risky.

There are two types of IPOs:

Start-up IPO:

This is a company that was not before the IPO. In other words, entrepreneurs come together and create a business plan. To obtain the financing required for the company, they decide to publish the information immediately by contacting the investment banker. If an investment banker believes this is a good concept, they will seek financing through an IPO.

Public-Private Company: An IPO for a company that exists for seeking the capital for expansion. The company has long been a small private company but decides to raise funds to achieve more during the IPO.

Before investing in Small-Cap Companies:

❖ Keep in mind two points when investing in stocks:

❖ The company should be well established.

❖ The company is profitable.

These positions are particularly important for investors in small stocks. Many startups lose money but hope to get rich in the future. The biotechnology industry is the best example. Biotechnology is an interesting area but esoteric and at this early stage, companies struggle to use the technology profitably.

Investing in small-cap stocks requires analysis

Small caps are also their risk appetite, like large caps. They also compensate for the risk, compensate you for more information about yourself and the interested share collection. Large-cap stocks protect information because they are vast. Smaller stocks get less press and control.

Keep in mind the given points:

Understand your investment style.

Small-cap stocks may have more potential benefits but are also associated with a higher risk. No investor should allocate most of their capital to low capitalization stocks. If you're considering retirement, you'd better invest in large-cap stocks, exchange-traded funds (ETFs), investment-grade bonds, bank accounts, and mutual funds. For example, the retirement benefit should be invested in investments that are either very secure or have been proven to show sustainable growth in the long term (five years or more).

Check with SEC. Receive the financial statements that the company must file with the SEC. These reports provide more complete information about the activities and finances of the company. Visit the SEC website at www.sec.gov and check out the extensive company registration database in EDGAR (Electronic Data Collection, Analysis and Retrieval System.

Investing for Income

Investing for income means investing in stocks used to make money. While profitable stocks do not offer outstanding growth, they are good for a steady flow of money.

Profitable stocks may be suitable for many investors, but are particularly suitable for the following Individuals:

Novice and conservative type of investors: Conservative investors want a slow but steady approach to growing their money and receive regular dividend controls.

Retired individuals: Growth investments are best suited for long-term needs, while profitable investments are best suited for current needs. Retired individuals may want some growth in stocks but are more interested in having a regular income that can keep up with inflation.

Dividend reinvestment plan investors: For those investors who like to compound their money with DRPs, income stocks are perfect.

Understanding Income Stocks

When people talk about making money on stocks, they usually talk about dividends. A dividend is nothing more than the money paid to the owner of a share. You buy dividends mainly for earnings, not for impressive growth potential.

Dividends are reported on an annual basis but are usually paid quarterly. For example, if a stock pays a dividend of $ 4, you are likely to pay $ 1 per quarter. In this example, if you have 200 shares, you would receive $ 800 per year or $ 200 per quarter. A regular review of dividends every three months can be a good advantage. A stock with a good return is a stock with a dividend above the average. It cannot be guaranteed that dividend rates will rise or fall, or in some extreme cases, dividends may be set. Fortunately, most companies that pay dividends continue to operate indefinitely and increase dividend payments from time to time. Historically, dividend growth has reached inflation.

Advantages of income stocks

Profitable stocks are usually one of the least volatile stocks, and many investors consider them defensive stocks. Protective stocks are stocks of companies that sell goods and services that are normally needed regardless of the economic form. Food drinks and utilities are excellent examples of countermeasures. Even if the economy is going through difficult times people still have to eat, drink and turn on the lights. Companies that offer relatively high dividends are usually also large in established, stable industries.

Some industries are known for their shares with high dividends. Utilities (such as electricity, gas and water), real estate investment trusts (REIT) and the energy sector (oil and gas) are places where you can find income. You can find high dividend stocks in other sectors but you will find their high concentration in these sectors.

Disadvantages of income stocks

Profitable stocks can fall like all stocks. You don't mind your income increasing in value, but it can fall just as easily. Factors that affect stocks in general politics, economic trends, changes in the industry, etc. also affect stocks of companies. Fortunately, equity returns have not suffered as much as other stocks when the market declines as high dividends tend to support stock prices. As a result, the profit prices of stocks in a falling market tend to fall less than the prices of other stocks.

The sensitivity of Interest rate

Stock returns may be sensitive to rising interest rates. As interest rates rise investments become more valuable. When your profitable stocks return 4 per cent and interest rates rise to 5 per cent, 6 per cent or higher. As more and more investors sell their stocks at a low-interest rate, the prices of these stocks are falling. Another important point is that raising interest rates can affect the financial stability of the company. In turn, if a company has to pay more interest which may affect its results and dividends.

Inflation eats into dividends

Although many companies regularly increase their dividends, some do not. Or if they do increase their dividends, the increase can be small. If income is your main consideration, you want to know this. Suppose you have one XYZ share at $ 10 a share with an annual dividend of 30 cents. Inflation means that you're spending increases; Inflation reduces the value of your dividend income. Conservative investor income can be exposed to various types of risk.

Analyzing Income Stocks

You choose stocks of income mainly because you want or need the income now. As a secondary point, income stocks have the potential for sustained long-term growth. Therefore, if you invest in retirement needs that will not be realized within 20 years income stocks may not be suitable for you to invest in growth stocks as they are more likely to make your money grow faster than your long-term investment   term.

If you are sure you want to get profitable stocks to do an approximate calculation to determine how much of your portfolio you want to borrow for profitable stocks. Suppose you need $ 25,000 investment income to meet your current financial needs.

If you have bonds that bring you $ 20,000 in interest income and you want the rest to come in the form of dividends on profitable stocks you need to choose stocks that bring you $ 5,000 a year. If you still have $ 80,000 to invest in, you know that you need a portfolio of stocks that generate $ 5,000 in return, or 6.25% of the return.

Take the following table as an example for understanding the need for income.

Item	Your Amounts	Sample Amounts
A. How much annual income do you need?		$10,000
B. The value of your portfolio		$150,000
C. Yield necessary to achieve		6.7%

Income can be found by dividing item A by item B

From this simple table, you know that with stocks worth $ 150,000 and a 6.7% return, you will get an income of $ 10,000. If you are happy with that $ 10,000 and inflation is zero for the foreseeable future, then you have a point.

Unfortunately, inflation is likely to remain with us for a long time. Fortunately, you will benefit from sustainable income-oriented growth.

If you have profitable shares and you do not need dividends immediately, you should reinvest dividends in the company's shares. Each investor is an individual. If you are unsure of your current or future needs it is best to contact a financial planner.

Calculating yield

Because profitable stocks pay dividend income, you need to evaluate which stocks can bring you the most income. When choosing profitable stocks, the most important thing to consider is profitability. Taking the dividend yield of stock into account is the quickest way to find out how much money you will make from a particular stock compared to other stocks that pay dividends.

The dividend yield is calculated as follows:

Dividend yield = dividend income /stock investment

Checking the stock's payout ratio

You can use the payout ratio to find out what percentage of the company's profit is paid in the form of dividends. Please note that companies pay dividends on net income. Thus, the profit of the company should always be higher than the dividends that the company pays. To calculate the payout ratio:

Dividend / Earnings = Payout Ratio

Assume that Cash-Flow Now, Inc. (CFN) has $ 1 million in annual income. The total dividends must be paid out of $ 500,000 and the company has 1 million shares outstanding. Based on these numbers, you know that CFN has EPS of $ 1.00 and pays an annual dividend of 50 cents per share. The payout ratio is 50 per cent.

This number is a good payout ratio because even if the total profit of the company falls by 10 or 20 per cent, there is still ample opportunity to pay dividends. People who are concerned about the security of their dividend income should regularly monitor the payout ratio. The maximum allowable payout ratio should be 80 per cent, and a good range is from 50 to 70 per cent. A payout ratio of 60 per cent or less is considered very safe.

When a company faces significant financial difficulties, its ability to pay dividends is compromised. So if you need dividend income to pay your bills, you know the payout ratio better. Generally, a payout ratio of 60 per cent or less is certain.

Diversifying your stocks

If most of your dividend income comes from shares in one company or industry, you should redistribute your investments so as not to store all your eggs in one basket. Diversification concerns both income and growth stocks.

Examining the company's bond rating

The company bond rating is very important for equity investors. The bond rating gives an impression of the company's financial stability. Bonds are rated for quality for the same reasons that consumer agencies value products such as cars or toasters. Standard & Poor's (S & P) is the largest independent rating agency that reviews bond issuers.

Consider the following points to understand the ratings:

➤ If the bond rating is good, it means that the company is strong enough to fulfil its obligations. These liabilities include expenses, debt payments and declared dividends. When a rating agency gives a company a high rating, this is a good sign for those who hold the company's debt or receive dividends.

➤ If the rating agency downgrades the rating for bonds, it means that the company's financial stability worsens the red flag for everyone who owns bonds or company shares. A lower bond rating today can cause problems for dividends later.

➤ If the bond rating is not very good, the company will fight to fulfil its obligations. If the company cannot fulfil all its obligations, it must choose which one to pay. A repeatedly financially disadvantaged company preferred to reduce dividends or not pay dividends at all.

Exploring Some Typical Income Stocks

Practically every industry has stocks that pay dividends; some industries have more stocks that pay dividends than others. You won't find too many dividend-paying stocks in the computer or biotechnology industry! This is because these types of companies need a lot of money to fund expensive research and development (R&D) for new product development. Without research and development, the company will not be able to develop new products to stimulate sales, growth and future profits. Computers, biotechnology and other innovative industries are better for growth investors.

Utilities

Utilities generate high cash flow. Cash flow includes money from income and other items. This cash flow is required to cover expenses, loan payments and dividends. Utilities are the most common type of stock and many investors have at least one. Investing in your local utility company is a good idea. This makes paying electricity bills less painful. Before investing in utilities, consider the following:

Make sure that the utility's bonds are rated higher. Utilities tend to have good cash flow; don't be too concerned if the ratio reaches 70 per cent. If the utility covers an area that's doing well and offers an increasing population base area than it becomes well for your stock.

Real estate investment trusts (REITs)

Real estate investment funds (REIT) are a special type of share. REIT is an investment in which there are elements of both a public limited company and an investment fund.

This is similar to a share in the sense that it is a company whose shares are publicly traded on major stock exchanges. It has the usual features you'd expect from stocks that can be easily bought and sold through a broker, and earnings are granted to investors in the form of dividends etc.

REIT is like a mutual fund in that it does not make money selling goods and services. In the case of REIT, he makes money by buying, selling and managing his investment portfolio. The portfolio is full of real estate investments. It brings rental income and rental income, like any landlord. Besides, some REITs have their mortgages and generate interest income.

REITs are referred to as trusts only because they meet the requirements of the 1960 Asset Management Act. This law exempts REITs from income tax and capital gains tax if they meet certain criteria, such as sharing 95 per cent of their net income to the shareholders. There are other criteria, but profitable investors are interested.

Advantages of investing in REITs include the following:

➢ Unlike other types of real estate investments, REIT is easy to buy and sell. You can buy REIT by calling a broker or by visiting the broker's website, just as you can buy stocks. REITs have above-average returns. Since they must pay shareholders at least 95 per cent of their income, their dividends usually bring from 5 to 12 per cent.

➢ REIT is less risky than buying real estate directly. Since you are investing in a company that buys the property, you do not have to worry about the ongoing management of the facilities that manage the company. Typically, REIT doesn't just manage one property. It is diverse in a portfolio of different properties. The investment in REIT is available to small investors. REIT stocks are usually traded in the $ 10 to $ 40 range, which means you can invest with very little money.

➢ REIT has flaws. You have the same risks as with direct investment in real estate. Real estate investment reached a record level between 2000 and 2004, which means a recession is likely. Whenever you invest in an asset (real estate and therefore REIT) that has already taken off due to artificial stimulants, potential losses can compensate for potential income.

If you're looking for a REIT for investment, analyze it just like real estate. Look at the location and type of property. If California malls thrive and your REIT California malls buy and sell, you will succeed. However, if your REIT invests in office buildings nationwide and the office building market is overloaded and you also have difficult times.

Royalty trusts

The oil and gas sector has aroused great interest in recent years, as people and enterprises see much higher energy prices. Oil and gas prices have risen to record highs due to many bullish factors, such as rising international demand from China and other developing industrial countries. Some high-income investors have benefited from this price increase by investing in energy company shares, known as royalty trusts.

A royalty trust is companies that own assets such as oil and or gas-rich land and receive high fees from companies seeking access to these properties for exploration purposes. The commissions paid to royalty trusts are then paid out to their shareholders as high dividends. In the second half of 2005, dividend-paying royalty trusts generated revenue of the order of 8 to 12 per cent which is very tempting for other assets such as bank accounts and bonds, given the low returns over the decade.

Investors with less than $10,000

If you need to bet $ 10,000 or less on stocks, you should consider a mutual fund rather than individual stocks, as that amount of money may not be enough to properly diversify. However, if you plan to invest such a small amount, you should spread it equally across two to four stocks in two different sectors that look strong for the foreseeable future. Protective industries are for small investors.

Since $ 10,000 or less is a small amount in the world of equity investments, you may have to buy odd lots. Suppose you buy four stocks and they all cost $ 50 per share. If you invest $ 10,000, you will not receive 100 shares.

You may need to consider investing $ 2,500 per share, which means you end up buying only 50 shares of each share. If you buy an odd lot or near it, find out if the company has a dividend reinvestment plan (DRP) and use the dividends you earn to buy more shares.

Avoid the temptation to participate in IPOs, penny stocks and other speculative issues. Participation in them can be cheap, but the risk is too high for inexperienced investors.

Investors with $10,000–$50,000

If you have between $ 10,000 and $ 50,000, you have more options for investment diversification. Consider buying five to six stocks in three different sectors. If you're a cautious type, defensive stocks are enough. For investors looking for growth then looks for industries in sectors that have shown strong growth.

Diversification does not mean that under no circumstances should you have all of your shares in one sector. It's up to you. For example, if you have worked in a specific area all your life and are familiar with this sector, a stronger presence is good because your great personal knowledge compensates for the risk. If you've been working in retail for 20 years and know the industry inside out, you probably know more about the good, bad, and ugly aspects of retail than most Wall Street analysts. Use your knowledge for greater profitability. However, you still should not invest all your money in this separate sector, as diversification remains vital.

Investors with $50,000 or more

If you need to invest $ 50,000 or more, you shouldn't have more than five to ten stocks in two or three different sectors. It is difficult to carefully track more than two or three sectors and best to maintain simplicity. For example, Warren Buffett was considered the greatest stock market investor of all time who had never invested in a website business because he didn't understand it.

He invests only in companies that he understands. If this strategy works for billionaire investors, it cannot be so bad for small investors. I propose investing in no more than seven shares, as there is something like excessive diversification. The more stocks you have, the harder it is to track them. As you have more inventories, you need to do more research, read more annual reports and news articles, and follow the business news from more companies. Even in the best of times, you need to monitor your stocks regularly as a successful investment requires hard work.

Consider hiring a personal manager. If you have $ 50,000 or $ 100,000, this might make sense. Let the financial planner transfer you and carefully weigh the benefits with costs. **Here are some points to consider:**

➤ Make sure the manager has a philosophy and approach that you agree with.

➤ Ask the money manager to give you a copy of your written investment philosophy. Find out if you are happy with the selection of stocks by the finance manager.

➤ Ask the money manager to explain their strategy.

➤ A good way to assess the success of a strategy is to ask the financial manager about her previous recommendations.

Knowing When to Sell

Buying stocks is relatively simple. However, selling stocks can be a painful decision for investors. But this is painful only in two cases: when you earned money on your stock and when you lost it. It sounds like a bad joke, but it is not far from the truth.

The idea of selling stocks as they grow is related to the following issues:

Tax consequences: This is a good reason to think about a sale.

Emotional luggage: "This stock has been in our family for years." Believe it or not, investors point to this personal reason for torturing the sale of securities. **The following is a list of questions that investors should consider when selling stocks that have lost money:**

Tax breaks: This problem is a good reason to consider selling shares.

Proud: The best investors in history have made bad investments. Losing pride is cheaper than losing money.

Doubt: When an investor buys a stock for $ 50 and it reaches $ 40, he often believes that the stock bounces off immediately upon sale and reaches $ 60 and then kicks him. This can happen but usually, the stock price drops.

Fear of separation: "But I have had this supply for so long that it has become a part of me." People hold on to the loss of stocks for various illogical reasons. It's great to be married to someone; being married on sticks is ridiculous. If the promotion does not help your goals, it harms your goals.

People have a lot more reason to be tormented by selling bad stocks. However, you can learn to manage stock sales in a disciplined manner. **There are only two reasons to think about selling stocks, whether the stock price has risen or gone:**

➢ You need money. If you need money for a good reason, for example, to pay off your debts, pay a tax bill or buy a house, you need money. This reason is easy to see. Regardless of investment or tax considerations, stocks are there for you. I hope that you are engaged in financial planning, so you do not need to sell your shares for such expenses, but you cannot avoid unforeseen expenses.

➢ The stock no longer worked the way you wanted it to. If the action does not serve your goals of increasing wealth or achieving your investment goals, it is time to get rid of it and continue with the next action.

Trailing stops facilitate the sale of stocks if all else has not changed; you should not sell a share of the profit. Keep it as long as possible. But when it stops being a winning share, you sell it. If you don't know how and when to sell it, apply for a stop loss 5 or 10 per cent below market value and let the market take its course.

Understanding Brokerage Orders and Trading Techniques

Investment success is not only about choosing growing stocks. It is also about how you do it. Investors often think that a good choice of stocks means that you do your homework and then buy (or sell) it. However, you can go even further to maximize profits (or minimize losses). As an investor in stocks, you can use the methods and services available through your standard brokerage account. All the data warned me about it, and no doubt it was time to be careful. Investors didn't have to trust me, but they could (at least) use trailing stops and other methods to ensure greater investment success.

Investors who used stop-loss orders avoided the loss of trillions of dollars in equity losses:

- ❖ Checking Out Brokerage Orders
- ❖ Stockbroker orders are of two categories:
- ❖ Time-related orders
- ❖ Condition-related orders

Check out both jobs because they are easy to implement and invaluable in creating wealth and saving it. Using a combination of orders, you can optimize your strategy to better control your investment.

Time-related orders

Time-based orders mean exactly:

The order has a time limit. Investors typically use these orders in combination with conditional orders. The two most common time-related orders are day orders and redemption orders (GTCs).

Day order:

A daily order is an order to buy a stock that expires at the end of this trading day. When you tell your broker: Buy BYOB, Inc. for $ 37.50 and place a daily order then you mean you want to buy stocks for $ 37.50. However, if the stock does not reach this price, your order will expire at the end of the trading day. BYOB can trade for $ 39 but you don't want to buy it at that price because you don't think the stock is worth it.

As a result, you will have no problems keeping stock on that day. Daily orders depend on your preferences and personal circumstances. It may appear to you as if you do not want the specified order to remain outside of today's market promotions. You may want to check the price. In this case, a daily order is an ideal strategy. If you make a transaction and don't specify the time when placing an order, most brokers automatically consider it a daily order.

Good-till-cancelled (GTC)

An order awaiting cancellation is the most frequently requested customer. Although GTC orders are time-dependent, they are always associated with one condition, for example, B. when the stock reaches a certain price. A GTC order only means what it says: the order remains in effect until it is completed or until the investor cancels it. Although an order implies that it can work indefinitely, most brokers have a limit of 30 or 60 days (or more). At this point, the broker cancels the order or contacts you to find out if you want to extend it. Ask your broker about their specific guidelines.

A GTC order is usually associated with conditional or conditional orders. Suppose you want ASAP Corp. shares. Buy, but not at the current price of $ 48 per share. You did your homework on stocks, including value for money, value for money, and so on. I would do it for only $ 36 to buy per share. You choose the best bet and ask your broker to place a "$ 36 GTC order". This request means that your broker will buy stocks when they reach $ 36. Just make sure your account has funds to complete the transaction.

Terms and conditions of orders are very useful, so you should read the recommendations of your broker. Meanwhile, ask if there are any fees. Many brokers do not charge a commission for T&C orders, because if they result in a purchase (or sale) order, they generate a regular commission, like any exchange transaction. Other brokers may charge a small fee.

For becoming successful with GTC orders you need to know the following points:

<u>Want to buy:</u> In recent years, people have tended to buy stocks without thinking about what they can do to get more for their money. Some investors don't understand that the stock market can be the place for buyers looking for bargains. If you are ready to buy a high-quality pair of socks for $ 16 at a department store, but the seller says that the same socks will go on sale for only $ 8 tomorrow, the same applies if you are an economical consumer with stocks. Suppose you want to buy SOX, Inc. Priced at $ 26, but now it's priced at $ 30. You think $ 30 is too expensive, but you like to buy stocks for $ 26 or less. However, they don't know whether the stock will move at the desired price today, tomorrow, next week, or even next month. In this case, the order of terms and conditions is appropriate.

When did you want to sell: If you bought some socks at a department store and you discovered that they have holes and stock's price starts to unravel then you will be able to get rid of it. You may already own SOX (for example, $ 25), but fear that market conditions may reduce the price. You are not sure in which direction the action will move in the coming days and weeks. In this case, an order to sell shares at a certain price is a suitable strategy. Since the stock price is $ 25, you can place a sell order if it drops to $ 22.50 to avoid further losses. In this example, the GTC is also a time interval and accompanies the condition.

Condition-related orders

The order assigned to the condition means that the order is only executed if a certain condition is met. Conditional orders increase your ability to buy stocks at a lower price, sell them at a better price, or minimize potential losses. If the stock markets become bearish or uncertain, conditional orders are strongly recommended. A limit order is a good example of conditional orders. In the final order, it can be said: "Buy Mojeski Corp. for $ 45."But if Mojeski Corp. wasn't worth $ 45 then the job didn't run.

Market orders

When you buy stocks, the easiest way to order is to buy or sell stocks at the current best market price. It's that easy. Here is an example: Kowalski, Inc. Available at a market price of $ 10. If you call your broker and tell him to buy 100 shares "in the market", the broker completes the order for your account and you pay $ 1000 plus a commission.

I say the moment when there is the best affordable price because the price of shares is constantly changing and getting the best price may depend on the ability of the broker to process the purchase of shares.

In the case of very active stocks, a price change can occur within a few seconds. Often three brokers place orders for the same share at the same time and receive three different prices due to the broker's different capabilities.

The advantage of a market order is that the transaction is processed immediately and you receive your stock without having to worry about whether it reaches a certain price. For example, if you buy Kowalski, Inc. Due to the market order, you know that at the end of this phone call (or visiting the website) you will be sure that you will receive shares. The disadvantage of a market order is that you cannot control the price you pay per share. Regardless of whether you buy or sell your shares, you may not know exactly what price to expect.

Stop orders

A stop order is a conditional order that instructs the broker to sell a certain stock only when the stock reaches a certain price. It acts as a trigger, and the stop order is converted into a market order for the immediate sale of shares. A stop-loss order should not take advantage of small, short-term changes in share prices. It is designed to help you protect most of your money when the market suddenly turns against your stock investment.

Suppose you are Kowalski, Inc., the stock price rises to $ 20 per share, and you want to protect your investment from a possible future market downturn. An $ 18 stop loss will force your broker to immediately sell the stock if it falls below $ 18. In this example, if the stock suddenly drops to $ 17, the stop loss order will still work, but the final sale price will be $ 17.

In a volatile market, you cannot sell stop loss at your exact price. However, since the order is automatically converted to a market order, the sale is completed and you prevent further stock decline. The main advantage of a stop-loss order is that it prevents a significant decline in your shares. This is a form of discipline that is important when investing to minimize potential losses. Selling fallen stocks can be painful for investors. However, when they don't sell, stocks often continue to fall as investors hold, hoping for a price recovery.

Most investors set a stop loss that is about 10 per cent lower than the market value of the stock. This percentage gives the stock a certain limit to the fluctuations that most stocks do in everyday life.

Trailing stops

Trailing stops are an important way of preserving wealth for experienced investors and can be one of your key strategies when using stop-loss orders. A trailing stop is a stop loss that is actively managed by an investor and is increased along with the market price of the share. The stop-loss order "pulls" the share price up. As the stop loss rises, it increasingly protects the value of the stock from falling.

A real-life example may be the best way to understand stops. Suppose you bought Lucent Technologies (LU) in 1999 for $ 25 a share. Once you have completed the purchase, you immediately asked your broker to place a stop loss for $ 22 and place an order before cancelling. Remember what you did.

You put a permanent security network under your stock. A stock may rise as high as the sky, but if it falls, the price of the stock will trigger a $ 22 market order.

 Your stock will be sold automatically, which will minimize your losses.

If Lucent receives $ 50 per share within a few months, you can call your broker and cancel your previous stop-loss order for $ 22 and replace it with a new (higher) stop-loss order.

This higher stop-loss price protects not only your initial investment of $ 20 but also most of your profit.

If time goes by and the stock price ends, you can continue the stop loss price and get a reserve of GTC. Now you know why it is called a trailing stop: it raises the price of stocks, like a giant tail. The whole way is always more than moving up.

William O'Neill founder of Investor's Business Daily suggests a trailing stop of 8 per cent below the purchase price. That is his preference. Some investors can set trailing stops at 20 or 25 per cent. Stop loss is desirable or desirable in any situation and depends on your experience, your investment objectives and market conditions. In most cases, stop-loss orders are reasonable, especially when the market appears uncertain.

A trailing stop is a stop loss that you actively manage. Stop Loss is valid until cancelled (GTC) and constantly follows the stock price as it grows.

Consider the following points for the successful implementation of trailing stops:

❖ Keep in mind that brokers don't usually automatically set trailing stops for you. You will not place any orders of any kind without your consent. It is your responsibility to choose the type of order. You can increase, decrease or cancel a trailing stop order at your discretion. However, you need to monitor your investments when significant movements occur to respond to the movement accordingly.

❖ Change the stop loss order if the stock price changes significantly. I hope you will not call your broker every time the stock moves 50 cents. Change the stop-loss order when the stock price moves by 10 per cent. If you are buying a stock for the first time, ask the broker to place a stop loss of $ 81. If the stock rises to $ 100, cancel the stop loss by $ 81 and replace it with $ 90. If the stock price moves to 110 dollars, change the stop-loss order to 99 dollars, etc.

❖ Check your broker's terms and conditions ordering guidelines. If your broker expires in an AGB order after 30 or 60 days, you should be aware of this. You don't want to risk a sudden drop in your stock price without protecting your stop-loss order. If your broker has a term of 60 days, keep this in mind so that you can extend the order by additional time.

❖ Control your stock. A trailing stop is not a technique to fix and forget. Monitoring your investments is vital. If the investment decreases, your stop loss will prevent further losses. If the stock price rises significantly, be sure to adjust the trailing stop accordingly. Keep increasing your safety net while your stock continues to grow. Part of stock monitoring knows the beta, which you can read about in the next section.

Using beta measurement

To be a successful investor, you need to understand the volatility of existing stocks. In volatility, this volatility is also known as beta stock. Beta is a quantitative indicator of the volatility of a particular stock with the general market. Beta specifically measures stock dynamics when S&P moves up or down 1%. Beta measurement is higher than the overall market, while a beta below 1 is less volatile. Some stocks are relatively stable in price movements others jump.

Looking at Well-Known Betas

Company	Beta	Comments
Exxon Mobile	.464	Less volatile than the market.
Cypress Semiconductor	3.287	More volatile than the market
Public Service Enterprise Group	.369	Statistically considered much less volatile than the market.

Given below table shows some sample betas of well-known companies.

You can find the beta version of the company on websites that usually contain a lot of financial information about the company, for example, B. on the Nasdaq website (www.Nasdaq.com) or Yahoo! Finance (Finance.yahoo.com).

Beta is useful because it gives you a general overview of the trading range of stocks. If the stock value is $ 50 and it trades in the range of $ 48 to $ 52, a trailing stop of $ 49 doesn't make sense. Your stock will likely be sold on the same day that you initiated the stop loss. If your stock is a volatile growth stock that can fluctuate up and down 10 per cent, you should be more logical to set your stop loss 15 per cent below that day's price. Most stocks in a mature industry tend to have low beta close to the general market. Shares of small and medium-sized companies in new or emerging industries tend to show great volatility in their daily price fluctuations. Therefore, they usually have a high beta.

Limit orders

A limit order is a very precise order in terms of terms, which means that the limit is either on the buy or sell side. You only want to buy (or sell) at the specified price or better. Limit orders work best for you when you buy a stock, but they may not work for you when you sell a stock.

Here's how it works:

When you buy: simply because you like a certain company and you want to receive its shares, this does not mean that you are ready to pay the current market price. You can buy Kowalski, Inc., but the current market price of $ 20 per share is not acceptable to you. You prefer to buy it for $ 16 because you think that the price reflects the real market value.

When the stock is highly volatile or drops to $ 16.01, it suddenly drops to $ 15.95. At the next step, you may be shocked to hear. Since your order was limited to $ 16, it can only be processed for $ 16, nothing more or less. The only way for this special deal is when the stock rises to $ 16. However, if the price continues to drop, your limit order will not be executed and may expire or be cancelled.

When you buy a stock, many brokers interpret the limit order as "buying at that particular price or better." If your limit order is to buy a stock for $ 10, you can also be happy if your broker buys this stock for you for $ 9.95. Thus, you will still receive a share at a lower price if you do not get exactly $ 10 because the price of the shares was volatile. Talk to your special broker to clarify the value of the limit order.

When selling: Limit orders are only activated when the stock reaches a certain price. For $ 20 and worry about lowering the stock price, you can place a limit order for $ 18. When you see and hear the news that Kowalski's price is falling, you can sigh and say, "I'm very glad I placed this limit order for $ 18". However, in a volatile market, the price of shares may exceed the price you specify. It can grow from $ 18.01 to $ 17.99 and then continue to decline. Since the stock price never reached $ 18, it is not for sale. Perhaps you are sitting at home, happy (wrongly) to play wisely while your stock drops to 15, 10 or fewer dollars! It is best to have a stop loss.

Buying on Margin

Margin means buying securities like stocks with funds that you borrow from your broker. Buying shares on margin is similar to buying a home with a mortgage. If you buy a house at a purchase price of $ 100,000 and fall 10%, your capital will be $ 10,000 and you will mortgage the remaining $ 90,000. If the value of the house rises to $ 120,000 and you sell, you will make a profit of 200 per cent. How so? A profit of $ 20,000 from this property represents an increase of 20% in the purchase price of $ 100,000. However, since your actual investment is $ 10,000 (down payment), your profit will increase to $ 200%.

Margin purchase is an example of using leverage to maximize profits with rising prices. Leverage means to borrow money to buy the stocks. This type of leverage is good in a cheap market, but it works against you in a bad market. For example, suppose a $ 100,000 home that you buy with a $ 90,000 mortgage drops to $ 80,000. Since you owe more than yourself, you still have a negative state. The lever is a double-edged sword.

Examining marginal outcomes

Suppose you believe that Mergatroid, Inc. shares, which are currently $ 40 per share, will gain in value. You want to buy 100 shares, but you only have $ 2,000. So you take an additional $ 2,000 from your margin broker.

If the stock price goes up

This result is best for you. When Mergatroid grows to $ 50 per share, your investment will cost $ 5,000 and your outstanding margin loan will cost $ 2,000. If you sell, the total loan proceeds will pay off and you will receive $ 3,000.

Since your initial investment was $ 2,000, your return is 50%, since your main amount of $ 2,000 ultimately turned into a profit of $ 1,000.

However, if you pay $ 4,000 in full without a margin loan, your $ 4,000 investment will bring you a profit of $ 1,000 or 25%. With the margin, you double the return on your money. Leverage, when used properly, is very beneficial. However, it is still a debt. So understand that you will ultimately have to pay them off, regardless of equity performance.

If the stock price fails to rise

If the stock is not going anywhere, you still have to pay interest on this margin loan. If the stock pays dividends, this money may cover part of the cost of the margin loan. In other words, dividends can help you repay your loans to the broker. If stocks don't go up and down, this appears to be a neutral situation, but you pay interest on a margin loan every day. For this reason, margin trading can be a good consideration for conservative investors when stocks pay high dividends. In many cases, high dividends on stocks of $ 5,000 can exceed the threshold percentage you have to pay out of the $ 2,500 (50 per cent) you borrow from a broker to buy those stocks.

If the stock price drops, a margin purchase may work against you. You don't see a disaster at this time, but you should be careful because the margin loan exceeds 50 per cent of your equity investment. If the value is lower, you can get a scary margin request when the broker contacts you and asks you to reconnect between the margin loan and the value of the securities. The next section provides information on the ratios of debt to equity.

Maintaining your balance

When buying margin stocks, you must maintain a balanced margin-to-equity ratio of at least 50%. If part of the debt exceeds this limit then you need to restore that ratio by depositing more shares. Additional shares you deposit may be shares transferred from another account.

For example, if Mergatroid grows to $ 28 per share, the margin loan share will exceed 50 per cent of the value of this stock - in this case, because the market value of your stock is $ 2,800, and the margin loan is still $ 2,000. Margin credit is 71 percent of market value ($ 2,000, divided by $ 2,800 = 71 percent).

If you can't find any more stocks, other securities, or cash, the next step is to sell the stocks from the account and use the proceeds to repay the margin loan. For you, this means a loss of capital - you have lost money on your investments.

The Board of Governors of the Federal Reserve System regulates the broker's margin requirements by Regulation T. T Rule prescribes the margin requirements that brokers present to their clients. For most of the listed shares, this is 50 per cent.

As you can see, the margin can increase your profits, but also your losses. If your stock falls, you can get a margin loan that exceeds the market value of the stock you bought earlier. In the emerging bear market from 2000 to 2002, stock losses have hurt many people, and a large number of those losses have worsened because people have been unable to meet margin trading commitments.

When you buy stocks on the edge, take a disciplined approach. Be especially careful when using leverage, such as margin loans, as they can have unpleasant consequences. Pay attention to the following points:

Have enough cash reserves in your account. Try to keep your margin ratio at 40 per cent or less to minimize the chance of a margin call.

If you're a beginner, you should use margins to buy stocks of large companies that have a relatively stable price and pay good dividends. Some people buy stocks with earnings whose dividend yield exceeds the interest rate on the margin, which means that the stock ultimately pays the margin loan. Just think of these stop commands.

Always keep an eye on your inventory. If the market turns against you, the result is especially painful if you use margin. You have a depreciation plan for margin debt. Margin loans for your investments mean that you pay interest. Your ultimate goal is to make money, and paying interest will affect your profits.

Going Short and Coming Out Ahead

The vast majority of equity investors are familiar with buying stocks, holding them for some time and hoping their value will increase. Such thinking is termed long-term, and long-term investors are considered to hold shares. A long position essentially means that you are optimistic and take your profit from rising prices.

However, smart investors also benefit from the market when share prices fall. Buying stocks is a common technique for capitalizing on falling prices. Investors made big profits in the bear market, taking short positions. Short selling is a bet on the fall of a particular stock. To make short sales, you must be classified as creditworthy. Your account must be approved for short sales. If you are approved for margin trading, you are likely to also make a short sale. Talk with your broker about your account restrictions regarding short positions.

Since a short position carries more risk than a long position, I strongly advise inexperienced investors to avoid short positions until they become more experienced. Most people easily understand how to make money when you are away for a long time. Going short means making money by selling high and then buying low stocks.

It can be difficult to think about this saying in the opposite direction. The short-stroke mechanism is very simple. Consider an example that the fictional company DOA, Inc. uses. As a share, DOA ($ 50 per share) looks pretty painful. He has a lot of debt and sales and revenue have dropped sharply, and there is news that the DOA industry will face difficult times in the foreseeable future. This situation describes a stock that is an ideal candidate for the purchase. The future may be boring for DOA, but promising for experienced investors.

You must understand the rules of the broker before making short sales. The broker must allow you to do this, and you must comply with the minimum security requirements, which are usually $ 2,000 or 50 per cent of the market value of short stock. When a stock brings dividends, these dividends are paid to the owner of the stock, and not to the person who lends it for sale.

Setting up a short sale

Suppose you think DOA is the right advertisement for short positions - you are almost certain that the price will drop. With a $ 50 DOA, you instruct your broker to "make 100 short stocks on DOA". Here's what happens next:

Your broker takes 100 DOA shares either from him or from another client or broker.

It is right. Customer may borrow shares without approval. The broker guarantees the transaction, and the client/owner of the share should never be informed, as he never loses the legal and beneficial right to the share. You borrow 100 shares and return 100 shares after the transaction is completed.

In your account for $ 5,000 (100 shares × $ 50) - the money you get from selling shares borrowed. You have to pay interest. You buy your legality.

When it is time to complete the transaction, you need to return the number of borrowed shares (in this case, 100 shares). If you buy back 100 shares for $ 40 per share, and these 100 shares will be returned to their owner, you will receive a profit of $ 1,000.

Going short when prices grow taller

I bet you suspected the remarkable profitability of selling shorts has a disadvantage. Suppose you made a mistake in DOA and the stock price went up from $ 50 to $ 87. You still have to return the 100 borrowed shares. If the stock price is $ 87, it means you have to buy it for $ 8,700. Well, you have that initial $ 5,000 in your account as soon as you open a short position in stocks. But where do you get the rest of $ 3,700 ($ 8,700 less than the original $ 5,000)? You have to cough up the difference. If the stock continues to grow, it's a big cough.

Short trade may be riskier than a long one. If you go for a long time, you can lose a maximum of 100 per cent of your money. However, if you miss, you may lose more than 100 per cent of the money invested.

Since you have no chance of losing if you take a short position, I recommend using a stop order to minimize the damage. Better yet, make the order pending, as I mentioned earlier in this chapter. You can set a stop order at a specific price. When the stock reaches that price, buy the stock back to return to the owner before the price goes higher. You still lose money, but you limit your losses.

Watching out for ticks

Sellers of short positions should be aware of the rules of the upward tick, according to which you can close short positions only if the stock has just grown. In this case, "tick" means the actual gradual movement of the price of the stock you are selling. For a stock of $ 10, which was only $ 9.95, a difference of 5 cents means an increase.

If the stock at $ 10 was only $ 10.10, the difference of 10 cents is a downtrend.

The number of ticks does not matter. So if you opened a short position at $ 40, the immediate previous price should be $ 39.99 or less. The reason for this rule (regulation of the Federal Reserve System) is that short selling can exacerbate falling share prices in a rapidly falling market. In practice, a short position, the price of which is already falling, could lead to a further decline in the share price. Excessive short sales can make the stock more volatile than usual.

Feeling the squeeze

When you sell a short stock, keep in mind that sooner or later you will have to buy that stock back so that you can return it to the owner. All of these short sellers are trying to buy back stocks so they can complete their deals before losing too much money. This massive purchase accelerates stock growth and puts pressure on investors who have reduced stocks (the so-called short squeeze).

Short maybe a good manoeuvre in a falling market but it can be brutal if the stock price goes up. If you are a beginner, avoid short sales until you have enough experience to take risks.

Ten Challenges and Opportunities for Stock Investors

The economic/political environment, stocks may be the best (or worst) investment. The stock market is confronted with many economic problems, including what happens to government policies, social trends, and national/international geopolitical conditions.

You should be aware of the "big picture" by regularly visiting such great websites as Financial Sense (www.financialsense.com), Free Market News Network (www.freemarketnews.com) and Mises Institute (www.mises.org).

Debt, Debt, and More Debt

In early 2005, the US gross domestic product (GDP) reached $ 12 trillion. Great! However, the country's total debt reached $ 38 trillion. What has kept and growing the economy over the past eight to ten years has been huge and ubiquitous debt. Debt in almost every category is at record levels. The problem is that due to bankruptcy, these debts either have to be repaid or liquidated.

Both will have negative effects on the economy. Either stocks in general and/or your portfolio, in particular, can be seriously damaged. Make sure you are dealing with your duty now. Companies that have too much debt are at high risk. If the company drowns, your stock will follow. If the company goes bankrupt, the value of your stock will evaporate.

Derivatives

Derivative financial instruments are the largest financial market in the world. As of July 2005, the total value in US dollars will exceed $ 280 trillion. It easily overshadows the global economy. With ease! Now you don't need to understand them anymore, but you should know what can go wrong when a problem with derivatives occurs. The once-powerful Enron quickly fell apart mainly due to the tragic mistakes in its derivatives portfolio. Over the past 10 to 15 years, derivative "accidents" have shaped the financial landscape and could potentially seriously damage the stock market.

Real Estate

Just as several years ago everyone was in love with stocks and overdoing it, this also applies to real estate in 2004. The craze for real estate has become a dangerous bubble and a threatening economic development.

The expansion of the money supply, the excessive growth of lending and debt and the decrease in lending standards have become rocket fuels for the real estate market and have led to higher prices than reasonable market values. Millions of homeowners, investors and speculators will be affected. And listen, I'm not just talking about the owners. The tentacles of a real estate bubble extend far beyond brick and mortar. Hundreds of billions of mortgages were packed and resold as securities and acquired by many mutual funds, insurance companies, Fortune 500 companies and pension plans. Since the vast majority of them are "inferior" (risky) debts, this poses major problems when interest rates rise, the economy falls, and so on. The message is clear to you that make sure you have a mortgage under your control and your debts are manageable. Make sure you avoid stocks that are overexposed to a bubble that could overshadow the 1998-2002 stock bubble.

Inflation

The last time inflation was a serious problem in the late 1970s and the market was going through tough times. Interest rates rose to over 18 per cent, and these were economic problems for everyone. Even though inflation was typically held back in the 80s and 90s, it shows the resumption of life in this decade due to the massive expansion of the money supply, which started seriously in 1995. I think this is a small scandal that the official inflation rate excludes the cost of food and energy. Without food and energy, the inflation rate has recently fluctuated between 2.5% and 3%. Just think: until you eat, turn on the light or drive, everything is in order! If these costs were taken into account, the inflation rate would be two to three times higher.

For equity investors, this means that growing your money is more important than ever. When choosing stocks and understanding of the harmful effects of inflation should be considered. Some stocks will suffer while others will thrive.

Pension Crisis

You saw all the headlines: "Pension plans are a growing crisis." "San Diego Pension Crisis" "People live longer." "People are not saving enough for retirement." Many state / local governments and large corporations will experience financial difficulties in meeting their retirement plan obligations. At least millions of people will not receive as much as they expect when they retire.

n addition, Pension Guarantee Corporation does not have sufficient resources to cover the company's lack of pension plans. According to a survey by Forbes magazine, 313 (62%!) Of the 500 companies included in the S&P 500 do not have sufficient funds to cover their future expected financial obligations (as of early 2005). America is not alone; Europe, Japan and even China are in the same position.

The idea is clear: people need to save and invest more to close financial gaps that seem inevitable. Equity works well for long-term needs such as retirement savings. Start now because the future can sneak up on you faster than you think.

Government's Unfunded Liabilities

Social security and medical care will undoubtedly be gigantic challenges in the coming decades. In June 2005, total liabilities for these gigantic programs exceeded $ 44 trillion. This is an overall responsibility that is almost four times higher than our country's gross domestic product (GDP). Current beneficiaries will most likely not be affected, but anyone under the age of 65 will certainly be. We live longer than ever and in our older years; we have to be more proactive in our responsibility. For more information, contact the Social Security Administration (www.ssa.gov) and Medicare (www.medicare.gov).

Recession/Depression

History tells us that it is best to avoid equity investments during a recession or depression. Declining economic growth always follows an artificial economic boom.

In this decade, the likelihood of a recession or depression is extremely high, because it is necessary to solve economic problems and imbalances, which means a significant decline.

In economically difficult times, the best stocks are defensive because people buy these things no matter how good or bad the economy is. Cyclical stocks are suppressed, so it might be a good idea to look for real values after an economic turn. In the meantime, be careful and protect your money with reputable, financially sound companies. Use protection strategies with your money.

Commodities

A clever man once said, "The story cannot be repeated, but it can often rhyme." This decade is reminiscent of the 1970s in many ways. The equities experienced terrible times when inflation, the energy crisis and international tensions escalated. However, it was a good time to invest in energy, precious metals and goods. Gold and silver reached record highs at the end of the decade. Equity investors who have acquired stocks in these specific industries have made huge profits. The lesson we need to understand is that the conditions of this decade offer opportunities for natural resources that reflect the end of the 1970s. China and India are also growing, and they will need more raw materials for their growing economies and populations.

Energy

The global appetite for energy has brought prices to record highs, and the coming years promise even greater demand. The energy markets have seen a sea of change that makes current conditions far more diverse and serious than in recent decades. We have entered the era of "peak oil", which means that cheap and easily accessible energy is a thing of the past. In August 2005, oil reached $ 67 per barrel, as gasoline exceeded $ 3 per gallon in many places across the country. Suddenly, oil for $ 100 and gas for $ 7, it seems, is not so far. Nowhere is supply and demand more evident than in the global energy market.

For stock investors, this means at least the opportunity to raise your money directly or indirectly. If we want our prosperity to grow, we need to understand how energy affects our portfolios.

Try a resource like energy speculator Doug Casey (www.caseyresearch.com) for extensive information on the energy sector.

Dangers from Left Field

You can even make minor changes that can protect or increase your assets. Regardless of whether healthcare stocks flourish in response to new threats or health problems or stocks of companies that thrive on internal security concerns, your stock investment program can survive and flourish. Be aware and understand that successful equity investments do not occur in a vacuum.

CPSIA information can be obtained
at www.ICGtesting.com
Printed in the USA
LVHW080119171020
668893LV00004B/517

9 781801 092326